Book Title

Author _____   Nationality _____

Genre _____   Year _____   Pages _____

Memorable Quote	Page Number

Characters

Plot Summary

Notes

Rating ☆ ☆ ☆ ☆ ☆

Book Title

Author _____ Nationality _____

Genre _____ Year _____ Pages _____

Memorable Quote	Page Number

Characters

Plot Summary

Notes

Rating ☆ ☆ ☆ ☆ ☆

Book Title

Author

Nationality

Genre

Year

Pages

Memorable Quote	Page Number

Characters

Plot Summary

Notes

Rating ☆ ☆ ☆ ☆ ☆

Book Title

Author

Nationality

Genre

Year

Pages

Memorable Quote	Page Number

Characters

Plot Summary

Notes

Rating ☆ ☆ ☆ ☆ ☆

Book Title

Author _____ Nationality _____

Genre _____ Year _____ Pages _____

Memorable Quote	Page Number

Characters

Plot Summary

Notes

Rating ☆ ☆ ☆ ☆ ☆

Book Title

Author   Nationality

Genre   Year   Pages

Memorable Quote	Page Number

Characters

Plot Summary

Notes

Rating ☆ ☆ ☆ ☆ ☆

Book Title

Author _____ Nationality _____

Genre _____ Year _____ Pages _____

Memorable Quote	Page Number

Characters

Plot Summary

Notes

Rating ☆ ☆ ☆ ☆ ☆

Book Title

Author

Nationality

Genre

Year

Pages

Memorable Quote	Page Number

Characters

Plot Summary

Notes

Rating ☆ ☆ ☆ ☆ ☆

Book Title

Author

Nationality

Genre

Year

Pages

Memorable Quote	Page Number

Characters

Plot Summary

Notes

Rating ☆ ☆ ☆ ☆ ☆

Book Title _____

Author _____ Nationality _____

Genre _____ Year _____ Pages _____

Memorable Quote	Page Number

Characters

Plot Summary

Notes

Rating ☆ ☆ ☆ ☆ ☆

Book Title

Author   Nationality

Genre   Year   Pages

Memorable Quote	Page Number

Characters

Plot Summary

Notes

Rating ☆ ☆ ☆ ☆ ☆

Book Title

Author _____ Nationality _____

Genre _____ Year _____ Pages _____

Memorable Quote	Page Number

Characters

Plot Summary

Notes

Rating ☆ ☆ ☆ ☆ ☆

Book Title

Author

Nationality

Genre

Year

Pages

Memorable Quote	Page Number

Characters

Plot Summary

Notes

Rating ☆ ☆ ☆ ☆ ☆

Book Title

Author　　　　　　　　　　　　　　Nationality

Genre　　　　　　　　　　　　　　　Year　　　　　　　　　　　　　Pages

Memorable Quote	Page Number

Characters

Plot Summary

Notes

Rating ☆ ☆ ☆ ☆ ☆

Book Title

Author

Nationality

Genre

Year

Pages

Memorable Quote	Page Number

Characters

Plot Summary

Notes

Rating ☆ ☆ ☆ ☆ ☆

Book Title

Author

Nationality

Genre

Year

Pages

Memorable Quote	Page Number

Characters

Plot Summary

Notes

Rating ☆ ☆ ☆ ☆ ☆

Book Title

Author

Nationality

Genre

Year

Pages

Memorable Quote	Page Number

Characters

Plot Summary

Notes

Rating ☆ ☆ ☆ ☆ ☆

Book Title

Author

Nationality

Genre

Year

Pages

Memorable Quote	Page Number

Characters

Plot Summary

Notes

Rating ☆ ☆ ☆ ☆ ☆

Book Title

Author

Nationality

Genre

Year

Pages

Memorable Quote	Page Number

Characters

Plot Summary

Notes

Rating ☆ ☆ ☆ ☆ ☆

Book Title

Author   Nationality

Genre   Year   Pages

Memorable Quote	Page Number

Characters

Plot Summary

Notes

Rating ☆ ☆ ☆ ☆ ☆

Book Title

Author   Nationality

Genre   Year   Pages

Memorable Quote	Page Number

Characters

Plot Summary

Notes

Rating ☆ ☆ ☆ ☆ ☆

Book Title

Author
Nationality
Genre
Year
Pages

Memorable Quote	Page Number

Characters

Plot Summary

Notes

Rating ☆ ☆ ☆ ☆ ☆

Book Title

Author

Nationality

Genre

Year

Pages

Memorable Quote	Page Number

Characters

Plot Summary

Notes

Rating ☆ ☆ ☆ ☆ ☆

Book Title

Author _____ Nationality _____

Genre _____ Year _____ Pages _____

Memorable Quote	Page Number

Characters

Plot Summary

Notes

Rating ☆ ☆ ☆ ☆ ☆

Book Title

Author

Nationality

Genre

Year

Pages

Memorable Quote	Page Number

Characters

Plot Summary

Notes

Rating ☆ ☆ ☆ ☆ ☆

Book Title _____

Author _____   Nationality _____

Genre _____   Year _____   Pages _____

Memorable Quote	Page Number

Characters

Plot Summary

Notes

Rating ☆ ☆ ☆ ☆ ☆

Book Title

Author

Nationality

Genre

Year

Pages

Memorable Quote	Page Number

Characters

Plot Summary

Notes

Rating ☆ ☆ ☆ ☆ ☆

Book Title

Author   Nationality

Genre   Year   Pages

Memorable Quote	Page Number

Characters

Plot Summary

Notes

Rating ☆ ☆ ☆ ☆ ☆

Book Title

Author _____   Nationality _____

Genre _____   Year _____   Pages _____

Memorable Quote	Page Number

Characters

Plot Summary

Notes

Rating ☆ ☆ ☆ ☆ ☆

Book Title

Author   Nationality

Genre   Year   Pages

Memorable Quote	Page Number

Characters

Plot Summary

Notes

Rating ☆ ☆ ☆ ☆ ☆

Book Title

Author _____ Nationality _____

Genre _____ Year _____ Pages _____

Memorable Quote	Page Number

Characters

Plot Summary

Notes

Rating ☆ ☆ ☆ ☆ ☆

Book Title

Author   Nationality

Genre   Year   Pages

Memorable Quote	Page Number

Characters

Plot Summary

Notes

Rating ☆ ☆ ☆ ☆ ☆

Book Title

Author

Genre

Nationality

Year

Pages

Memorable Quote	Page Number

Characters

Plot Summary

Notes

Rating ☆ ☆ ☆ ☆ ☆

Book Title

Author Nationality

Genre Year Pages

Memorable Quote	Page Number

Characters

Plot Summary

Notes

Rating ☆ ☆ ☆ ☆ ☆

Book Title

Author

Nationality

Genre

Year

Pages

Memorable Quote	Page Number

Characters

Plot Summary

Notes

Rating ☆ ☆ ☆ ☆ ☆

Book Title

Author

Nationality

Genre

Year

Pages

Memorable Quote	Page Number

Characters

Plot Summary

Notes

Rating ☆ ☆ ☆ ☆ ☆

Book Title

Author

Nationality

Genre

Year

Pages

Memorable Quote	Page Number

Characters

Plot Summary

Notes

Rating ☆ ☆ ☆ ☆ ☆

Book Title

Author   Nationality

Genre   Year   Pages

Memorable Quote	Page Number

Characters

Plot Summary

Notes

Rating ☆ ☆ ☆ ☆ ☆

Book Title

Author   Nationality

Genre   Year   Pages

Memorable Quote	Page Number

Characters

Plot Summary

Notes

Rating ☆ ☆ ☆ ☆ ☆

Book Title

Author

Nationality

Genre

Year

Pages

Memorable Quote	Page Number

Characters

Plot Summary

Notes

Rating ☆ ☆ ☆ ☆ ☆

Book Title

Author

Nationality

Genre

Year

Pages

Memorable Quote	Page Number

Characters

Plot Summary

Notes

Rating ☆ ☆ ☆ ☆ ☆

Book Title

Author   Nationality

Genre   Year   Pages

Memorable Quote	Page Number

Characters

Plot Summary

Notes

Rating ☆ ☆ ☆ ☆ ☆

Book Title

Author _____ Nationality _____

Genre _____ Year _____ Pages _____

Memorable Quote	Page Number

Characters

Plot Summary

Notes

Rating ☆ ☆ ☆ ☆ ☆

Book Title

Author   Nationality

Genre   Year   Pages

Memorable Quote	Page Number

Characters

Plot Summary

Notes

Rating   ☆ ☆ ☆ ☆ ☆

Book Title

Author

Nationality

Genre

Year

Pages

Memorable Quote	Page Number

Characters

Plot Summary

Notes

Rating ☆ ☆ ☆ ☆ ☆

Book Title

Author   Nationality

Genre   Year   Pages

Memorable Quote	Page Number

Characters

Plot Summary

Notes

Rating ☆ ☆ ☆ ☆ ☆

Book Title

Author   Nationality

Genre   Year   Pages

Memorable Quote	Page Number

Characters

Plot Summary

Notes

Rating ☆ ☆ ☆ ☆ ☆

Book Title

Author

Nationality

Genre

Year

Pages

Memorable Quote	Page Number

Characters

Plot Summary

Notes

Rating ☆ ☆ ☆ ☆ ☆

Book Title

Author _____ Nationality _____

Genre _____ Year _____ Pages _____

Memorable Quote	Page Number

Characters

Plot Summary

Notes

Rating ☆ ☆ ☆ ☆ ☆

Book Title

Author

Nationality

Genre

Year

Pages

Memorable Quote	Page Number

Characters

Plot Summary

Notes

Rating ☆ ☆ ☆ ☆ ☆

Book Title

Author

Nationality

Genre

Year

Pages

Memorable Quote	Page Number

Characters

Plot Summary

Notes

Rating ☆ ☆ ☆ ☆ ☆

Book Title _____

Author _____   Nationality _____

Genre _____   Year _____   Pages _____

Memorable Quote	Page Number

Characters

Plot Summary

Notes

Rating ☆ ☆ ☆ ☆ ☆

Book Title

Author

Nationality

Genre

Year

Pages

Memorable Quote	Page Number

Characters

Plot Summary

Notes

Rating ☆ ☆ ☆ ☆ ☆

Book Title

Author   Nationality

Genre   Year   Pages

Memorable Quote	Page Number

Characters

Plot Summary

Notes

Rating ☆ ☆ ☆ ☆ ☆

Book Title

Author _____   Nationality _____

Genre _____   Year _____   Pages _____

Memorable Quote	Page Number

Characters

Plot Summary

Notes

Rating ☆ ☆ ☆ ☆ ☆

Book Title

Author

Nationality

Genre

Year

Pages

Memorable Quote	Page Number

Characters

Plot Summary

Notes

Rating ☆ ☆ ☆ ☆ ☆

Book Title

Author

Nationality

Genre

Year

Pages

Memorable Quote	Page Number

Characters

Plot Summary

Notes

Rating ☆ ☆ ☆ ☆ ☆

Book Title _____

Author _____ Nationality _____

Genre _____ Year _____ Pages _____

Memorable Quote	Page Number

Characters

Plot Summary

Notes

Rating ☆ ☆ ☆ ☆ ☆

Book Title

Author _____ Nationality _____

Genre _____ Year _____ Pages _____

Memorable Quote	Page Number

Characters

Plot Summary

Notes

Rating ☆ ☆ ☆ ☆ ☆

Book Title _____

Author _____ Nationality _____

Genre _____ Year _____ Pages _____

Memorable Quote	Page Number

Characters

Plot Summary

Notes

Rating ☆ ☆ ☆ ☆ ☆

Book Title

Author

Nationality

Genre

Year

Pages

Memorable Quote	Page Number

Characters

Plot Summary

Notes

Rating ☆ ☆ ☆ ☆ ☆

Book Title

Author _____   Nationality _____

Genre _____   Year _____   Pages _____

Memorable Quote	Page Number

Characters

Plot Summary

Notes

Rating ☆ ☆ ☆ ☆ ☆

Book Title

Author _____ Nationality _____

Genre _____ Year _____ Pages _____

Memorable Quote	Page Number

Characters

Plot Summary

Notes

Rating ☆ ☆ ☆ ☆ ☆

Book Title

Author

Nationality

Genre

Year

Pages

Memorable Quote	Page Number

Characters

Plot Summary

Notes

Rating ☆ ☆ ☆ ☆ ☆

Book Title

Author   Nationality

Genre   Year   Pages

Memorable Quote	Page Number

Characters

Plot Summary

Notes

Rating ☆ ☆ ☆ ☆ ☆

Book Title

Author _____ Nationality _____

Genre _____ Year _____ Pages _____

Memorable Quote	Page Number

Characters

Plot Summary

Notes

Rating ☆ ☆ ☆ ☆ ☆

Book Title

Author   Nationality

Genre   Year   Pages

Memorable Quote	Page Number

Characters

Plot Summary

Notes

Rating ☆ ☆ ☆ ☆ ☆

Book Title

Author

Nationality

Genre

Year

Pages

Memorable Quote	Page Number

Characters

Plot Summary

Notes

Rating ☆ ☆ ☆ ☆ ☆

Book Title

Author   Nationality

Genre   Year   Pages

Memorable Quote	Page Number

Characters

Plot Summary

Notes

Rating ☆ ☆ ☆ ☆ ☆

Book Title

Author

Nationality

Genre

Year

Pages

Memorable Quote	Page Number

Characters

Plot Summary

Notes

Rating ☆ ☆ ☆ ☆ ☆

Book Title

Author

Nationality

Genre

Year

Pages

Memorable Quote	Page Number

Characters

Plot Summary

Notes

Rating ☆ ☆ ☆ ☆ ☆

Book Title

Author _____ Nationality _____

Genre _____ Year _____ Pages _____

Memorable Quote	Page Number

Characters

Plot Summary

Notes

Rating ☆ ☆ ☆ ☆ ☆

Book Title

Author   Nationality

Genre   Year   Pages

Memorable Quote	Page Number

Characters

Plot Summary

Notes

Rating ☆ ☆ ☆ ☆ ☆

Book Title

Author   Nationality

Genre   Year   Pages

Memorable Quote	Page Number

Characters

Plot Summary

Notes

Rating ☆ ☆ ☆ ☆ ☆

Book Title

Author   Nationality

Genre   Year   Pages

Memorable Quote	Page Number

Characters

Plot Summary

Notes

Rating ☆ ☆ ☆ ☆ ☆

Book Title

Author Nationality

Genre Year Pages

Memorable Quote	Page Number

Characters

Plot Summary

Notes

Rating ☆ ☆ ☆ ☆ ☆

Book Title

Author   Nationality

Genre   Year   Pages

Memorable Quote	Page Number

Characters

Plot Summary

Notes

Rating ☆ ☆ ☆ ☆ ☆

Book Title

Author

Nationality

Genre

Year

Pages

Memorable Quote	Page Number

Characters

Plot Summary

Notes

Rating ☆ ☆ ☆ ☆ ☆

Book Title

Author   Nationality

Genre   Year   Pages

Memorable Quote	Page Number

Characters

Plot Summary

Notes

Rating ☆ ☆ ☆ ☆ ☆

Book Title

Author

Nationality

Genre

Year

Pages

Memorable Quote	Page Number

Characters

Plot Summary

Notes

Rating ☆ ☆ ☆ ☆ ☆

Book Title

Author

Nationality

Genre

Year

Pages

Memorable Quote	Page Number

Characters

Plot Summary

Notes

Rating ☆ ☆ ☆ ☆ ☆

Book Title

Author   Nationality

Genre   Year   Pages

Memorable Quote	Page Number

Characters

Plot Summary

Notes

Rating ☆ ☆ ☆ ☆ ☆

Book Title

Author

Nationality

Genre

Year

Pages

Memorable Quote	Page Number

Characters

Plot Summary

Notes

Rating ☆ ☆ ☆ ☆ ☆

Book Title

Author   Nationality

Genre   Year   Pages

Memorable Quote	Page Number

Characters

Plot Summary

Notes

Rating ☆ ☆ ☆ ☆ ☆

Book Title

Author

Nationality

Genre

Year

Pages

Memorable Quote	Page Number

Characters

Plot Summary

Notes

Rating ☆ ☆ ☆ ☆ ☆

Book Title

Author

Nationality

Genre

Year

Pages

Memorable Quote	Page Number

Characters

Plot Summary

Notes

Rating ☆ ☆ ☆ ☆ ☆

Book Title

Author   _____   Nationality   _____

Genre   _____   Year   _____   Pages   _____

Memorable Quote	Page Number

Characters

Plot Summary

Notes

Rating   ☆ ☆ ☆ ☆ ☆

Book Title

Author

Nationality

Genre

Year

Pages

Memorable Quote	Page Number

Characters

Plot Summary

Notes

Rating ☆ ☆ ☆ ☆ ☆

Book Title

Author   Nationality

Genre   Year   Pages

Memorable Quote	Page Number

Characters

Plot Summary

Notes

Rating ☆ ☆ ☆ ☆ ☆

Book Title

Author

Nationality

Genre

Year

Pages

Memorable Quote	Page Number

Characters

Plot Summary

Notes

Rating ☆ ☆ ☆ ☆ ☆

Book Title

Author   Nationality

Genre   Year   Pages

Memorable Quote	Page Number

Characters

Plot Summary

Notes

Rating ☆ ☆ ☆ ☆ ☆

Book Title

Author

Nationality

Genre

Year

Pages

Memorable Quote	Page Number

Characters

Plot Summary

Notes

Rating ☆ ☆ ☆ ☆ ☆

Book Title

Author

Nationality

Genre

Year

Pages

Memorable Quote	Page Number

Characters

Plot Summary

Notes

Rating ☆ ☆ ☆ ☆ ☆

Book Title

Author   _____   Nationality   _____

Genre   _____   Year   _____   Pages _____

Memorable Quote	Page Number

Characters

Plot Summary

Notes

Rating ☆ ☆ ☆ ☆ ☆

Book Title

Author

Nationality

Genre

Year

Pages

Memorable Quote	Page Number

Characters

Plot Summary

Notes

Rating ☆ ☆ ☆ ☆ ☆

Book Title

Author

Nationality

Genre

Year

Pages

Memorable Quote	Page Number

Characters

Plot Summary

Notes

Rating ☆ ☆ ☆ ☆ ☆

Book Title

Author

Nationality

Genre

Year

Pages

Memorable Quote	Page Number

Characters

Plot Summary

Notes

Rating ☆ ☆ ☆ ☆ ☆

Book Title

Author

Nationality

Genre

Year

Pages

Memorable Quote	Page Number

Characters

Plot Summary

Notes

Rating ☆ ☆ ☆ ☆ ☆

Book Title

Author

Nationality

Genre

Year

Pages

Memorable Quote	Page Number

Characters

Plot Summary

Notes

Rating ☆ ☆ ☆ ☆ ☆

Book Title

Author Nationality

Genre Year Pages

Memorable Quote	Page Number

Characters

Plot Summary

Notes

Rating ☆ ☆ ☆ ☆ ☆

Made in United States
North Haven, CT
31 May 2024